Endangered and Extinct Reptiles

Jennifer Boothroyd

Lerner Publications Company
Minneapolis

For Makenna
—J.B.

Lerner Publications Company
A division of Lerner Publishing Group, Inc.
241 First Avenue North
Minneapolis, MN 55401 U.S.A.

For reading levels and more information, look up this title at www.lernerbooks.com.

Library of Congress Cataloging-in-Publication Data

Boothroyd, Jennifer, 1972–
    Endangered and extinct reptiles / by Jennifer Boothroyd.
        pages — (Lightning bolt books™ — animals in danger)
    Includes index.
    ISBN 978–1–4677–1334–4 (lib. bdg. : alk. paper)
    ISBN 978–1–4677–2497–5 (eBook)
    1. Rare reptiles—Juvenile literature. 2. Extinct reptiles—Juvenile literature. 3. Reptiles—
Juvenile literature. 4. Endangered species—Juvenile literature. I. Title.
    QL644.7.B67 2014
    597.9168—dc23   2013022642

Manufactured in the United States of America
1 — PC — 12/31/13

Table of Contents

Reptiles

Reptiles are a group of animals. They have backbones. They have cold blood. Scales cover their bodies.

Iguanas and snakes are reptiles.

The tiger chameleon is endangered.

Endangered Reptiles

The short-nosed sea snake lives in the ocean. It eats fish and eels.

Not many of these reptiles are left in the wild.

Short-nosed sea snakes are from Australia. They swim in coral reefs.

The short-nosed sea snake's habitat has been damaged.

The hawksbill turtle has a pointed nose. This reptile finds food in coral reefs.

The hawksbill turtle's shell has many colors. Hunters catch these turtles to sell their shells.

Hunters have caught too many hawksbill turtles. This animal is endangered.

This jewelry is made from turtle shells. Refusing to buy turtle shell jewelry is one way people help hawksbill turtles.

Look at those sharp teeth!

The Chinese alligator lives in wetlands. A wetland is ground covered with water.

Swamps and marshes are wetlands.

This reptile has a strong tail.
The tail helps the alligator swim.

Laws protect these endangered alligators from hunters.

The Panay monitor lizard
lives in the Philippines.
It climbs high in trees.

This endangered
reptile eats
fruits and leaves.

This monitor lizard has skinny toes.

Each toe has a large, curved claw at the end.

This reptile is called a blue iguana.
Can you guess why?
It can turn bright blue!

Blue iguanas are endangered. People have harmed this lizard's habitat.

Blue iguanas sleep in caves or under rock piles. They spend days lying in the sun.

These iguanas are usually bluish gray.

Extinct Reptiles

Diplodocus is extinct. That means it has completely died out. No one knows why some reptiles died out.

Diplodocus lived millions of years ago.

People study this reptile's fossils. Fossils are hardened remains of animals or plants.

Diplodocus used its teeth to pull leaves off branches.

Allosaurus walked on two legs. It had two arms. It had a very long tail.

This animal's tail could be 17 feet (5 meters) long.

Allosaurus was a carnivore.

It hunted other animals for food.

Allosaurus had sharp teeth and claws. It died out millions of years ago.

This tough-looking reptile is an ankylosaurus. It became extinct 65 million years ago.

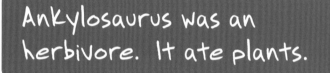

Ankylosaurus was an herbivore. It ate plants.

Flat plates covered this reptile's whole back. This animal's tail was strong and bony.

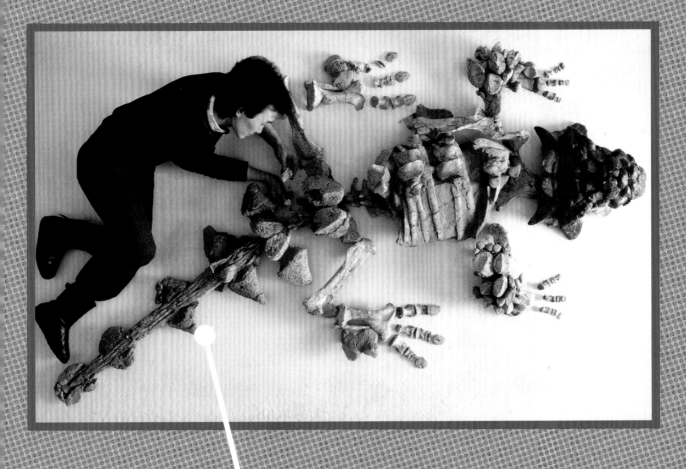

Ankylosaurus used its tail for protection.

Quetzalcoatlus was a huge flying reptile. Its wingspan was 40 feet (12 m) wide.

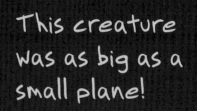

This creature was as big as a small plane!

Quetzalcoatlus had strong, thin bones.

This flying reptile has died out.

It could fly very far.

Navassa iguanas have been extinct for more than 125 years.

They lived on Navassa Island.

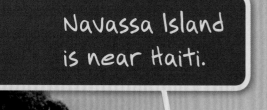

Navassa Island is near Haiti.

Mining damaged this lizard's habitat. The iguana died out.

These ruins were mines on Navassa Island.

Helping Endangered Reptiles

Many people are trying to help endangered reptiles. A wildlife refuge is a safe home for endangered animals. Refuge workers protect the animals.

Refuge workers and helpers put hawksbill turtles back into the wild.

Some endangered reptiles were put at risk from too much hunting and trapping. Trappers sold the reptiles as pets. New laws stop stores from selling endangered animals. If you see an endangered reptile for sale, don't buy it!

This leopard gecko is a good pet. It is not endangered.

27

What You Can Do

There are many things you can do to help endangered reptiles.

- Clean up trash from land and water. Reptiles need clean homes to stay healthy.

- Ask your parents not to use chemicals on your lawn or garden. Chemicals can get into wetlands. This can make animals sick.

- Learn more about reptiles. Read books or study reptiles online.

- Visit zoos and wildlife refuges. These places protect reptiles.

A Remarkable Recovery

Not all endangered animals die out. Antiguan racers used to live all over Antigua Island. By the 1900s, these snakes had disappeared. Rats were hunting the snakes. People had accidentally brought the rats to the island on ships. The Antiguan racer was believed to be extinct. Luckily, some were found on Great Bird Island in 1989. Many groups worked together to save the snake from extinction. The Antiguan racer is still endangered. But its numbers are growing.

Glossary

carnivore: an animal that eats other animals

endangered: at risk of dying out

extinct: died out

fossil: hardened remains of animals or plants

habitat: where an animal lives

herbivore: an animal that eats only plants

reptile: a cold-blooded animal with a backbone and scales. Reptiles breathe air.

scale: a thin, flat body covering

wetland: ground that holds a lot of water. Swamps and marshes are wetlands.

wildlife refuge: a protected place for animals to live

Further Reading

Heos, Bridget. *What to Expect When You're Expecting Hatchlings*. Minneapolis: Millbrook Press, 2012.

Hoare, Ben, and Tom Jackson. *Endangered Animals*. New York: DK Publishing, 2010.

Hughes, Catherine D., and Franco Tempesta. *First Big Book of Dinosaurs*. Washington, DC: National Geographic Books, 2011.

National Geographic Kids: Wildlife
http://kids.nationalgeographic.com/kids/animals/creaturefeature

Natural History Museum of London: Dinosaurs
http://www.nhm.ac.uk/kids-only/dinosaurs

San Diego Zoo Kids: Reptiles
http://kids.sandiegozoo.org/animals/reptiles

Silverman, Buffy. *Do You Know about Reptiles?* Minneapolis: Lerner Publications, 2010.

Index

Photo Acknowledgments

The images in this book are used with the permission of: © Corey A. Ford/Dreamstime
.com, p. 2; © Joe McDonald/CORBIS, p. 4; © Biosphoto/SuperStock, pp. 5, 30; © NHPA/
SuperStock, p. 6; © Sergio Pitamitz/CORBIS, p. 7; © Isabellebonaire/Dreamstime.com,
p. 8; © Louise Murray/Visuals Unlimited/CORBIS, p. 9; © Robin Winkelman/Dreamstime
.com, p. 10; © iStockphoto.com/Shoemcfly, p. 11; © Tim Laman/National Geographic/
Getty Images, pp. 12, 13; © iStockphoto.com/argalis, p. 14; © Mosnell/Dreamstime.com,
p. 15; © Pawel Libera/Loop Images/SuperStock, p. 16; © Francois Gohier/Science
Source, p. 17; © James Leynse/CORBIS, p. 18; © Image Source/Getty Images, p. 19;
© iStockphoto.com/Syldavia, p. 20; © Louie Psihoyos/CORBIS, p. 21; © Jonathan Blair/
CORBIS, p. 22; © Joe Tucciarone/Science Source, p. 23; U.S. Department of the Interior/
USGS, pp. 24, 25; © Yuli Seperi/Getty Images, p. 26; © Myrleen Pearson/Alamy, p. 27;
© John Cancalosi/Peter Arnold/Getty Images, p. 29.

Front Cover: © NHPA/SuperStock (top); © Isabellebonaire/Dreamstime.com (bottom).

Main body text set in Johann Light 30/36.